no, thank yo

JANINE AMOS

CHERRYTREE
BOOKS

A CHERRYTREE BOOK

This edition first published
by Cherrytree Books, part of
The Evans Publishing Group Limited
2A Portman Mansions
Chiltern Street
London W1U 6NR

Reprinted 2007

Printed in China

British Library Cataloguing in Publication data.

Amos, Janine
No, Thank You!. – (Good Manners)
1. Interpersonal relations – Juvenile literature
I. Title II. Spenceley, Annabel
395.1'22

ISBN 1 84234 306 8
13 digit ISBN (from January 2007) 978 1 84234 306 7

CREDITS
Editor: Louise John
Designer: Mark Holt
Photography: Gareth Boden
Production: Jenny Mulvanny
© Evans Brothers Limited 2005

With thanks to:
Holly Gill, Charlie Horwood,
Georgia Debank, Kiani Gordon,
Jayden Chalmers, Jordan Burke,
Sian and Taylar Wong

VISIT OUR WEBSITE
www.evansbooks.
Evans

Mum's Cake

It is teatime. Mum has made a cake.

Mum offers the cake to Charlie.

No.

The children forget to say thank you.
How does Mum feel?

Georgia smiles and says
No, thank you.

How does Mum feel now?

Too Busy!

Kiani is busy drawing.

14

Do you want to make paper planes with me?

Joshua comes over.

Kiani is busy.

No.

How does Joshua feel?

Joshua goes over to Jordan.

Building a Palace

Isobel is building a palace.

Katie comes over.

Shall I help you?

I only
wanted
to help!

How is Katie feeling?

Isobel thinks about it.

How does Katie feel now?

That's OK.

When you say No it can make your friends feel pushed away.

It may seem as if you don't care about them.

TEACHER'S NOTES

By reading these books with young children and inviting them to answer the questions posed in the text the childre
can actively work towards aspects of the PSHE and Citizenship curriculum.

Develop confidence and responsibility and making the most of their abilities by
- recognising what they like and dislike, what is fair and unfair and what is right and wrong
- to share their opinions on things that matter to them and explain their views
- to recognise, name and deal with their feelings in a positive way

Develop good relationships and respecting the differences between people
- to recognise how their behaviour affects others
- to listen to other people and play and work co-operatively
- to identify and respect the differences and similarities between people

By using some simple follow up and extension activities, children can also work towards

Citizenship KS1
- to take part in discussion with one other person and the whole class

Prospect Heights Public Library
12 N Elm Street
Prospect Heights, IL 60070
www.phpl.info

EXTENSION ACTIVITY
Circle Time
- Seat the children in a circle. Read the story of *Mum's Cake* and ask the children to contribute answers to the questions 'How does Mum feel?' and 'How does Mum feel now?'
- Pass an object such as a toy or stone around the circle. Only the person holding the object is allowed to speak. Ask the children to name one thing they love to eat.
- Going around the circle, turn pairs of children to face each other. Ask them to talk only to their partner. Remind the children of the story and ask them to discuss the reasons they think Holly and Charlie said no to the cake. After a minute ask the children to turn round again and share their ideas with the group.
- Ask the children to think about what Georgia did that changed how Mum felt.
- She said 'no, thank you'
- She gave her reason – she was full up
- Ask the children to give an example of a situation where they might say no (such as being asked to play out) and as each child speaks give them the talking object. After each contribution ask for the 'kind' response, e.g. 'No, thank you, I have to stay in on Wednesday'.
- Then, pass the object around the circle and ask each child to state one thing they have done well during the Circ Time such as listening, taking turns, talking to a partner, putting up their hand, sitting still, etc.

These circle time activities can be repeated on subsequent days with the other two stories in the book or with othe
stories from the series.